Let's Take a Vote

TAKING CIVIC ACTION

Seth Matthas

CIVICS FOR THE REAL WORLD™

Rosen Classroom™

Do you and your classmates ever have to choose between two things? This is a good time to take a vote!

Sometimes you might need to take a vote at school. By voting, students can let their teacher know what they want most.

You could vote on a class pet. Some students might want a fish. They can say why they think fish are good pets.

Other students might want a pet rabbit for the classroom. They can say why they think rabbits are good pets.

When everyone has the facts about rabbits and fish, your class can take a vote. Which class pet would you want?

You might take a vote about what snack to eat. You could have cookies or cupcakes. What snack will win the vote?

If more people want to eat cookies, then cookies will win the vote. Find out the winner by asking the whole class!

Your teacher may ask where to go on a class trip. You and your classmates can decide by taking a vote.

You can go to the farm or the zoo. If more students vote to go to the zoo, the zoo wins. Everyone still gets to see animals.

There are many things to vote on at school. Someday maybe your classmates will vote for you to be class president!

WORDS TO KNOW

cookie

cupcake

fish

rabbit